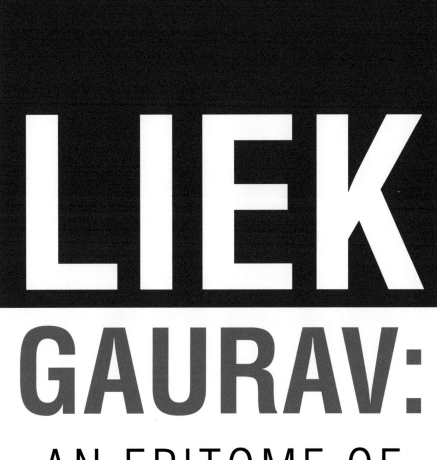

LIEK GAURAV:

AN EPITOME OF HARD WORK

Gaurav Soni

To order additional copies of this book, contact:
Xlibris
NZ TFN: 0800 008 756 (Toll Free inside the NZ)
NZ Local: 9-801 1905 (+64 9801 1905 from outside New Zea-land)
www.xlibris.co.nz
Orders@ Xlibris.co.nz

ISBN: Softcover   978-1-5434-9694-9
         EBook   978-1-5434-9693-2

Print information available on the last page

Rev. date: 11/12/2020

Contents

Chapter I

A Portrait of my Family

There are just so many countless experiences that one encounters in his or her life. However, out of these handfuls of experiences, there are a number of them that are important enough to have an impact on our lives and to leave memories. These moments could be negative or positive, depending on how we managed things in the past, how we think, how we feel, and how we exactly react. These experiences have contributed so much to what we are now and the people we chose to be part of our circle. They have taught us to be mentally, spiritually, and physically ready, growing up, and lead to our development as an individual. The important things that were taught to us when we were still kids had shaped us for what we have become today. We take such things to our heart, and look back to them, as we revisit every process of acting, reacting, and delivering when we get to face tough situations. Whether good or bad, the said experiences were also the backing factors to our identity.

I am somewhat feeling a kind of fear as I begin to write and share the very story of my life. This task, which is writing an autobiography, is a difficult one. I have to link the years in the past with the present. I will unveil to you my earliest impressions, joys and sorrows of childhood, and a lot of incidents that are of vital importance in my education. I will do my very best to present to you in a series of sketches, only the episodes that, for me, seem to be the most important and interesting. I will start off talking about the essence of family and how I gave value to where I came from.

Life, to me, means my family and my dreams. I preferred remembering the happy side of my life, but just any other person, I also have the so-called "days of." That simply means that I also had sad days. These days pertain to the days of struggles that I had to face, from childhood until adolescence stage that had contributed to who I am today. However, I also had beautiful memories, moments that are still fresh in my mind and heart.

> *"A joint family used to be... The joy and security of living in a joint family...love...cooperation...sacrifices...quarrels and unity of family members."*
>
> *-AnamiKasak*

Living in a joint family has always been a memorable one. Anyone could just imagine a house filled with kids running around, being happy with just a mat unfolded on the kitchen floor. More talking and more bonding moments surely happen. An extra dose of unconditional love, happiness, and support are surely felt coming from your grandparents, your parents, your uncles, and aunts, and also from your cousins and siblings. You get to do everything together in a fun and meaningful way, just like arranging things, cleaning your bedrooms, and washing the dishes. Sharing also becomes a way of caring when you live in a joint family, starting from dresses to food to gadgets and etc. It is also found out that people who came from a joint family have turned out to be more responsible, more caring, and more mature.

The system of having a joint family is very prevalent in India. It started from the Vedic times and was even made more popular when the Kings ruled the land. People prefer to be tied with a blood relation and opted to live in a single household because of so many personal reasons. Adjusting with all the family members like aunts, cousins, and uncles is part of the challenges in a big family. However, growing and learning together will always prevail.

I have been talking about family, specifically having a joint family from the start, since that is where I exactly came from. A type of family that I was accustomed to. I am personally writing this now to radiate inspiration and hard work to everyone out there who somewhat has the same story as I do.

Allow me to share my humble beginnings to all of you, my struggles and hardships but also, my triumph and experience. This is my story of hard work and perseverance in life. I will be sharing with you the significant experiences and people who became great contributors to my personality, and the challenges in life I had to go through to be who I am today, with my beautiful wife and my two lovely children here in New Zealand.

There is so much joy in living in a joint family. Studies have claimed that children who were born and came from a joint family are considered having the edge over those who are born and raised in nuclear families. I was more than blessed to be in a joint family, having my grandparents, aunts, uncles, cousins, and siblings around. I placed all my childhood moments in my long-term memory.

It seems like yesterday. It seems like days and years were just taken by a snap of a finger.

Everything happened so fast, without me realizing that I really have gone through a lot, and I am just so thankful that I made it. I was able to get out of poverty. I am now living the life I dreamed of having, years back.

Let me start my life story by introducing myself. I am Liek Gaurav. I was born on a warm, sunny day on the 18th of May in the year 1990. I came from a very, very small town up in the Himalayas in India. Yes, you heard it right, Himalayas. It is known to be Mount

Everest. The Himalayas that spreads across Bhutan, China, India, Nepal, and Pakistan. I have been a smart and hardworking little man since I was young. My parents and my entire family have molded me well and cultured me with good qualities. I am the youngest in the family of five, consisting of my mother, my father, and my two sisters.

This picture was taken when I was around 2 years old.

There are a lot of things I like, but there are a lot of things I do not like, as well. When

I was young, I liked to play with my cousins and siblings. I really wanted to have fun with them. Simple things already make us happy. I loved it when my parents made an effort to also get to have fun with us, sometimes. One of the things I don't like is getting muddy. There was one time my siblings threw some mud on me for fun, but for me, it was not fun at all.

Another thing I do not like is to just plan without putting things into action. I do not like that. That's is why whenever I have plans, I immediately write them on a paper so I could be guided on what to do first and put it into action right away. Well, by now, you might know some of my personalities, but the things I mentioned were just a seed in a tree. It is not everything. Allow me to start sharing more with you.

Growing up, I was surrounded by a good and prosperous family. I could say it is good. After all, we are raised well and prosperous because we achieved what we wanted because of working hard. We worked hard together. For me, my family is not just anything. They are everything to me. They are my inspiration as to why I worked hard and became my ideal self today. No family is perfect, there were times that things go well, there are also times that they don't.

Nonetheless, I loved where I came from. I lived in a joint family in the past. I mean, we lived in a bigger family, staying on a single household, together. Just like the bird's eye view, I included earlier about joint family, I was able to happily live in a joint family and experienced how to be in it. Living in a joint family, for me, has always been a noteworthy experience. The memories that we shared together were very priceless, and I could say they are irreplaceable. We lived in our grandmother's house. We were not rich, back then. My grandmother, my father's mother, has five boys, and these five boys settle for as a joint family with the eldest uncle, who is looking after others. Imagine, we were many in the family. From my grandparents, my uncles, my cousins, my aunts, and my siblings.

The house we lived in is quite spacious and classy. It was also not that elegant to look at. Our house was just simple, a strong reflection of the people living in there. Our house was never quiet and was never lonely. I mean, no dull moments happened. Kids were noisy, but not all the time. We played a lot. We loved to run outside and have a race. We had a rule that whoever reaches the assigned destination first, will be the winner and will be given a chance to give a dare to the losers. We also used to make kites and made them flew into the sky. Kites were just made out of plastic and other indigenous materials. Playing basketball also became part of our childhood games. Sometimes, we played it among ourselves, sometimes, still, there were also moments that my dad and my uncle joined, which even made our game more exciting and thrilling. We also helped our parents in doing household chores. More importantly, we studied hard, really hard. I had no time making fun of my studies. Even at a very young age, I already dreamt of a lot of things. When I see my father outside and doing things on his farm, I used to feel pity for him. How I wish my father did not have that kind of job. Every day, I get to witness how tired he is on the farm. He had to work hard for us. He worked like a carabao, tirelessly performing all his tasks. I am just also blessed to have a very supportive mother, in everything that my father does, she assisted and helped him. They are indeed a perfect match. My family lived a simple rural life. No fancy things are experienced. No expensive gadgets are played and held. No cars to brag about in school. Despite these absences, we were happy, genuinely happy. You could just create a whole picture in your mind that in the house, we shared one table for meals, our food was carefully and properly divided, we use the same bathroom, the same kitchen, and the same living room, so as other stuff. Though it's kind of crowded and messy to imagine, we were able to get along with it and get to embrace the situation that we were placed.

I was 7 years old during that time.

Talking about my uncles, they seemed to be the backbone of support and the pillar of our finances every single day. They have been very hardworking, too. My uncles were able to go overseas to Austria. I know that even if they were

not experiencing the kind of job that my father is having, their jobs were also not easy. They also had to exert effort and release sweat for it. Talking about my father, "poor in studies" became a short description, but he is very industrious in life. He was not smart in terms of academics. Fewer opportunities were given to him. He did try schooling, but he's got very low grades. Because of this, my father just followed the advice of his other brothers to stay at home, while they were overseas and looking for means to support the family. Sad to hear, right? But maybe they think it would be better for him to just stay home and look after the house and the land. But if they were to ask me of my opinion about this, and if I had the right to speak that time on my father's behalf, I would love to also see my father having a degree. I would love to see him have a successful life. Not all people are smart in school, but they are smart in other things. Maybe that is what my father has. For sure, my father also had a dream. I guess he is not just sharing with us because probably he's shy and he knew the whole time that he couldn't make it.

Nonetheless, I am still very proud of my father. He worked hard for us every day. His job may not be as classy as others, but being a farmer is also very noble. Other people depend on farmers for food, and I thank my father for providing such to us.

The three brothers, my uncles, went to Austria to work while the other one was left with us at home, being a teacher. The four of them landed on good jobs. On the other hand, my father did not. At home, my father used to have cows, goats, and all that stuff. His main goal was to produce good crops and also health animals to make a living for us. My father lived an ordinary life being a daily wage earner at home, while others are in Austria. One of them is a School Principal. A typical farmer's life was embraced by my father. Taking care of the animals, feeding the cows and goats and chickens, planting some vegetables, and looking after us. Daily, he gets up very early, specifically before sunrise, for him to be able to work on his field.

At the same time, everything is still fresh, and the ambiance is still not hot. He goes to the farm by walking because aside from the fact that we did not have a car before, the farm is never far from home. My father has spent his years in agriculture and already loved the said path. He was an expert on his own in terms of crops and animals. However, it takes time to earn something big out of the crops that he planted. Since I had lived in a joint family, we received money coming from our uncles. They always do that to support our needs, especially that my grandmother is already old. She needed money to buy her medicines. However, the money sent by our uncles were still, not enough. The eldest uncle of mine did not join us in the house and instead, lived separately but just pretty nearby. Only a few meters from the house. He built his own home there because his kids are all grown up. But, I could say we are still a joint family. We still have each other's back, and they always came to the house to visit us and bond with us.

Basically, going back to my father, to be direct to the point, he is not smart. He is just plain and clear. No complications. What he knows well is farming. He had to do well and strive harder because he had to feed a number of tummies. We are five in the family. Me, being the youngest in the family, and I have two elder sisters who helped me all throughout my journey. Since I am the youngest, more attention was given to me. And since I am the only thorn among the petals in the rose, my father always trained me of what to do and what to avoid. My father trained me to be more of a man, doing a lot of stuff, showing enough strength, being physically fit, and practiced me to become responsible. My father, not being able to finish his studies and not being able to get a good job, he had learned early and quickly the need to use effective resources. One thing I learned from both of them is to practice waking up early. My mother always told us to wake up as early as 5 in the morning and start our day with meaningful tasks. Not everyone is a morning person, so this became a good trait and to all of us and taught us to discipline in time. My parents also did not waver into reminding us to do great in our studies because, as they said, knowledge is the only thing that will not be stolen from us. Education and discipline are very important for them, and it was passed on to us, as I passed it on as well to my children. About food, since we are not rich, we only had to get and eat the food that we can possibly consume. We could not just waste food.

At home, while my mother stays home with us to take care of us, prepare meals for us, and discipline us, my father, who is very hardworking, spends all his day on the farm to look after the cows and comes home just to eat or sleep. My father, unlike my mother, is not very strict with rules. He just lets us do what we want to, we just have to be responsible for all our actions.

He even shared with me that before, when he was still young. He was not used to making assignments. While my other uncles were very busy making one, he said he tried hard reading his homework. Still, he somewhat had a lack of interest, and when he got to read more, he already felt bored. So, he did not bother anymore doing home works at all. He preferred playing outside the house even if my grandparents would scold him because of not doing his assignments. He would even get comparisons that his brothers were far way better than him. Still, he always answered that he really could not be as smart and studious as his brothers were. Going back, as I said, we had a schedule for making it. My sisters and I have to be together while doing home works. I could still remember that the clock already ticked at 7:30 in the evening, we already have to start making our tasks. My mother always instructs us that we should already be flipping our books, look into our notes, and start doing the tasks. Whenever we encounter lessons that we could not understand or anything that we could not find an answer, most especially the most difficult ones, I always asked for my uncle's assistance, my uncle, who is a school principal. However, when my sisters were in trouble looking for answers and forgetting about the formula or the clues, they would directly ask me. Of course, as a brother, I always helped them. Of the three of us, I am far way better than them in terms of academics, but I am not boasting. I am just frank with you, to them, and to myself. My sisters also knew that, since we were still kids. I would tell you more about it, later, when I get to share with you my schooling experiences. So, as I said, our mother would check us from time to I time if we're done or not. In terms of tutoring us, my father could not do that since he barely knows anything if it is about studies, so what he usually does is pure observation. After making our home works, we get to eat our dinner. My mother, while we were making our school stuff, was also very busy back then in the kitchen, preparing for our simple, but healthy and delicious home-cooked meals.

Our parents had instilled in our minds a lot of things. They shared with us, their children, all the struggles they encountered in the past, the difficulties they went through, and the trials they faced. These are the very reasons why, at the age of four, they already started training us, most especially me. They wanted us to know how to stand on our own, with or without them. My family, my mother, and my sisters could not have another man to stand for them. That is the very reason why, at a young age, my mother already passed to me some knowledge about life and how to handle things more sensibly and practically. She always told me to study hard for me to be able to reach my dreams.

My parents wanted me to become a professional. They wanted me to be on a path which I really dream of having. Maybe working in the office and have a good life in the near future. Even if my father is just as simple as that, I am more than proud of him. He became our strength, especially in times of problems. I know he felt bad for the times he could not provide everything for us, times when he needed to ask for support from his brother, and times when he thought of himself being a failure as a man. Well, my mother, too, but I could say they have been so good to us three. They were great parents. They have loved us unconditionally. They have trained us to be ready for the real world, ready for struggles, ready to not give up, and ready to rise up every time I fall in life. We are not rich. We are just fortunate to be able to eat three times a day. But compared with the other people in our area or town, we worked hard, most especially my parents every day for what to eat. We do that together. The value of togetherness was really given so much importance years back.

Growing up, I never felt lonely. I cherished little joys and achievements with all the family members that made everyone happier. My cousins were my playmates. Simple things can already make us happy. During my childhood life, I used to go to school together with my uncle because he used to be a School Principal. Kids went together to school by simply walking. My uncle kept teaching us a few things while we walked to and from school. I also kept asking about academics, especially about Science. This is one of the reasons why I learned a lot of things that apply to the real world now.

In terms of the financial aspect, money had always been a problem and an issue. Growing up, it has become a barrier to living a good life. Our family did not have much savings, most notably that we are many. My uncles sent us money, but still not enough. My father's earnings are also small, not enough as well. We could not buy anything we want or desire. What was given more priority is our daily needs. But of course, we were able to surpass things together, day by day. Things just really got them going since they handled everything rightly. My family was able to manage our financial issues and was able to make both ends meet as a family. The challenges we have been through became my motivation while growing up, that I should work hard to be able to provide well for the family in the near future. I want to be a good family man who knows how to protect and stand for my family. I do not want to fail them. Also, I greatly desire to help my parents and my entire family. I want to buy land and build a house. I want them to get out of poverty. At a very young age, my mindset was already like this. Full of aspirations in life. I was more than motivated to make a difference in my life.

Being in a big family, I gained a lot of values that my parents and uncles shared with me, and I was reared well, which is really evident in who I have become today. Each person in the family has portrayed a very significant role and contribution to all the family members. I was greatly influenced by how they act and treat one another. I learned the act of sharing. Since

I was surrounded by many people, I became more social but practiced a habit of sharing. It was inculcated to us since childhood. If ever I had food or anything, no matter how small or big it could be, I then distributed it among my siblings and to everyone in the house. That was what I also saw from them. Imitating and following their actions were really good.

I also acquired the value of respect. I developed it by observing his elders at home. I learned how to keep my tongue in check around elders, learned how to respect them, and learned how to obey their commands. I was also trained to be emotionally strong. It would be an advantage for children to be emotionally strong if they live in a joint family. It is because many people would be around for them. The elderly in the house also taught discipline to us. They told us moral stories, which helped us understood the very importance of having discipline in our lives. Love and care also were imprinted in my hearts. I was cultured that whenever someone is sick, proper care must be given to that person, just like what I always received from my loved ones when I get sick. I was also able to witness how my mother and father cared for and love each other. How my mother takes care of my father and how my father does the same. The love that I received from them was immeasurable. My mom also taught me the sense of responsibility quite early in my life. My mother used to give me phone bills and money to deposit. I practiced standing on the lane for it. Those times made me accomplish the qualities mentioned earlier. The upbringing that I got from my parents was really good.

On the other side of the coin, aside from the financial constraints, being in a joint family also caused some feuds, compromises, and sacrifices, which somewhat gave my family a big challenge. It is undeniable that sometimes, ideas just don't match and minds don't always agree, but also disagree. Privacy, for example, is compromised. Everyone in the family knows everything about all the members of the family, which caused interference in some matters. Hiding things became an option, especially when I felt sad or angry. I couldn't just let it all out because I was never alone in the house and will never be. Any small decision is also run by all. Any move required a go signal from all the members of the family, whether you like it or not. Living together is really difficult. In a joint family, a person has to put others' needs first before his or hers. However, these challenges and struggles make any person a better version of himself or herself, and that's what happened to me. In an innocent young mind comes a better self while growing and was ready to take all the hurdles that may arise.

Chapter II

School in the Province

Living in the province has been a dream of many. You get to enjoy the breathtaking natural sceneries. Life would be so relaxing and so far away from hustle sounds from cars or buses. Noise from many people will also be absent. Fresh air is also free when you wake up in the morning. Commuting is also made easier, and neighbors are friendlier. Prices of commodities are also cheaper compared to the city's standard prices. Lastly, life becomes more harmonious and peaceful.

Other pros of living in the province are the following: you get to avoid the breezy traffic. If you are the type of person who does not want the city traffic, which you cannot endure daily, then provincial life is the answer. In small towns almost non-existent traffic occurs. You get to have an extraordinary level of comfort. A breathtaking view will surely be enjoyed in the province. This is something which is considered a luxury when you are in the city. You get to also buy more for less in the province. The prices of the goods in the province, most especially those that are freshly produced, are much lower compared to the ones being sold in the city. This is because of the number of farms and farmers in the province. Fresh catch seafood is even offered at lower prices. The greens and the very fresh air are also embraced by people living in small-town areas. There are just lots of trees and vast green fields that would surely amaze you.

You cannot find these in the city. These make the air fresher and cooler. A concrete jungle idea is associated with city life. For nature lovers, provincial life is the perfect answer. Reuniting with nature in every beauty that it has is a great idea. Commuting is also made easier when you are in the province, so as navigating to places you want to be in. More so, you get to have neighbors that are friendlier and more caring.

The descriptions mentioned above are the things I enjoyed much back then. The green fields, the fresh air, the people, everything! I had a beautiful and simple provincial life. I grew up with the greeneries and the relaxing environment. All the noise I could hear is the noise coming from the animals around. No jeep, no bus, no traffic, no pollution. I lived in a healthy and peaceful environment, where every move does not need complications. Since my father is just a daily wage earner at home and has cows and goats for a living, I was exposed to farm life. I had also learned to live a simple life and enjoyed everything within our means. Doing chores also became part of my routine, so as to help my father on the farm like feeding the animals. My mother and father have instilled in our minds to dream big, no matter how hard it could be, in order to reach brighter a tomorrow and to not just settle on the kind of life we were experiencing. Early morning, we had to walk meters away from the house to fetch some water. After that, I had to help my father in feeding the goats and the cows. I needed to get more grasses from afar. My sisters were helping my mother in preparing for food, and they were doing the stuff for girls. My father and I also did chopping of woods. He also trained me on how to properly balance time. I mean, doing two or three tasks at the same time, without comprising the outcome or possible result of the task. That was our daily routine when there is no schooling. However, when we have to go to school, lesser tasks were given to us because we all prioritized schools as more important, but when we come home, we still get to help our parents do the chores.

Many people believed that the fortunate ones are those individuals who were born with a silver or gold spoon in their mouth. That simply means that they belong and that they come from a wealthy family. That also means they have everything. To be specific, it is true that they are very lucky and I guess, a chance to be envied. However, what could be luckier or I could say happier is to be born in a joint family, free and so gifted with the wealth of nature. I am talking about myself being born in a small town where the farm can be found. Living far away from crowded cities has become an escape for us. Our only source of living before mostly came from the natural resources we had around. We had no silver. We had no gold. What we had were only free useful things from nature that helped us live, as well. We had free water, free vegetables, free fresh air, and sometimes, free rice from the farm.

On our small farm, my father built a small hut. It is a small shelter that is where we usually find rest whenever we go to the farm and visit the animals we have there. It has become a symbol of the simplicity of life that we had in the past. Unlike in every city, it is very impossible to see big buildings, malls, or anything concrete there on the farm. I could still remember that there was free-flowing water near the farm, which also brought happiness to us when we were still young. My siblings, my cousins, and I used to take a shower there. We splashed water to each other's' faces. We waded in the free-flowing water with happiness. It was very cold, fresh, and clean. Clearwater, I should say. It was truly one of the most unforgettable moments of my life. The fresh air I was talking about earlier was also clean and healthy. The experience is quite far from those people living in silver spoons. They live in an air-conditioned room or house. Nothing beats inhaling and nourishing fresh and unpolluted air. When there's no class, going to the farm has always painted smiles on my face. I always get excited and thrilled. I was assigned by my father to pull weeds in the garden there. There were also some days he would ask me to water the plants. During summer, if there's no class, I could just walk outside and pick some fresh vegetables and bring them back home. I would directly give it to my mother because she was the one cooking in the house. Aside from she's mother, she's also good at cooking. My mother's meals are the best.

She's used to using fresh, home-grown ingredients at all costs. I was also able to build small fences when my father asked me to help him. We had to do it to replace the old and damaged fences. Our livestock, the goats, chickens, and cows were also taken care of well. I was involved in feeding and cleaning them. My father really showed me how to do such because he wanted me to grow, knowing everything you could do for a living. My sisters were, most of the time, with my mother. They were also doing their own craft. Most of the time, I was with my father, having a son and father bonding in little simple ways. I learned to appreciate everything about it because my father has taught us love for it since we were little. We learned to love simple living and great hard work. True enough, no one could compare a good and happy life in the caress of the farm. I often miss the peace and serenity brought by provincial life, as well as the sense of community and togetherness. There is truly a rich and special feeling to live a life in the province.

This was me when I was 9 years old.

The work and challenges we faced before in the province, I could still reminisce, most especially the hurdles faced by my parents. From raising us to feeding us, to disciplining us, and to provide our needs in life. I have seen them work without limitation, sacrifice without hesitation, and love without asking anything in return. They had given their own version of best for us.

One evening, I happened to come across a Chinese proverb that states, "Learning is a treasure that will follow its owner anywhere." In my own understanding and opinion, the saying tries to say that learning is looked at and considered to be a great treasure in which we do or should value greatly. What it means when your knowledge is a treasure that will follow its owner is how once you are of full knowledge of something, that knowledge that you gained will never ever leave you. I love this quote. I do. This quote reminds me to do well in my quest for education. It makes me realize how much I should value learning, knowing the fact that my parents never fully got the chance to get an education like I do. I have realized that even though we are not rich, and we were not enrolled in good and famous schools, I was still given the opportunity to study. I know there are many kids out there who wish to be able to study and reach their dreams in life. I was given a chance to have a better life than the others, who have not even know what it is to feel when you are in school. Seeing that my parents never got the chance to complete school, I felt as it is my responsibility, our responsibility, since my sisters were with me, to complete school. Also, not because it is what my parents expect of me and will make my family proud of me, but because it will be for my own good for my own future.

I firmly believe that education opens doors to opportunities. It has always been the key to success. It heals ignorance and plants knowledge. Education would even lift up any person from poverty. It also gives wisdom and power to every individual thirsty and hungry for a good future. It also binds understanding and communication. Lastly, it is the only treasure, the most expensive one, wrapped with gold and silver, which could not be taken away from you. In terms of schooling, I grew up to be a smart person. I am not bragging, just like what I shared earlier, but I was just honest, and my family knows that very well. When I was still young, I was schooling up north, together with my sisters. Life was never easy back then. So many struggles were needed to be taken and surpassed successfully. In school, we did not have the luxury of things. We just used what our family could provide. We did not always have new shoes. There was even a time that I had a pair of shoes repeatedly used for a couple of years, but most of the time, I just wore slippers. Our parents did not give us money to bring to school. We were only given food to eat. Whenever I get to see my classmates eating a good lunch or carrying great stuff, I just simply stared and said to myself that I can have those in the coming years when I get to have a stable job. We faced poverty at that time, but we were able to conquer it. Of course, when I was schooling, my uncle, who is a School Principal, always walked with us and taught us a lot of wonderful and useful things about academics and about life. He would ask us to do some mental calculations, remember some formula, require answers to riddles, and tell stories with us. My uncle also asked us the English names of some things. These were given out like a game. There was never a dull moment in going to school. Everything was filled with fun and enjoyment. I, together with my sisters, used to walk three to four kilometers in summer in the morning to school. You could just imagine the intensity of hotness brought by the scorching heat of the sun that penetrated into our skin. I also walked back in the rain, all walking on the foot. No buses are available during that time. Everywhere is reached through walking. I was used to it already. I did not like the sun much, but I so loved the rain. I felt like I am rejoicing while heading home. My family never heard me complain. I was just silent about our situation but was contemplating at the same time. Despite the said challenges, despite going to and from the school tired because of the heat and rain, I was still showing the qualities of being a smart kid. I was very eager to learn something new every single day. I made the poverty we are experiencing as my motivation. Whenever I walked with the heat and the rain, I was thinking of my parents. My struggles were very far from what they sacrifice just for us to be able to go to school. I even told myself before that I want to acquire a car in the future. So I need not walk a long way to wherever I like to be. I need not get soaked with the rain since there will be a shelter for me. I also wanted my parents to experience how it is to feel when you are riding in a car. So much childhood dreams were formulated.

In school, I was even pretty shocked in my studies; from the very start, I was a brainy guy. I got high scores in tests and performed well in school. My classmates always asked me what the answer to this is and what the answer to that is. My teachers always praised me for my performance. At home, I also got chances of teaching my sisters of their other subjects, especially those that they hardly understand. I am more than proud to say that I have always been part of the chosen few in the class to become one of the competitors in higher classes. At first, I was quite shy to face a lot of people, but my one teacher of mine approached me. He said to me that I am good. He also said that he saw great potential in me. Those words were so refreshing in my ears. Every time I faced other students, I just remembered what my teacher told me, and then my guts increased and increased. Among the many students in the class, I became part of the privileged. I enjoyed all the experience, learned a lot of things, and honed my knowledge more. What is even better is that I also used to teach my sister's classes. We get to enter the classes of my elder sisters, students who were older than us. We were like having tutorials, especially to those who needed assistance in terms of academics, and especially to subjects that they found difficult to understand and lessons that needed more explanation and comprehension. After every school year, my parents would receive recognition for me, for being one of the tops in class, and for being a good student. My sisters, on the other hand, were simply on the average, but they were also very happy for me and so supportive. They would always give applause whenever I get to enter their classroom, and other students would directly praise them for having a younger brother like me. Just very amazing to absorb for a young mind to already manifest such brilliance and gift of knowledge. All throughout my completion of learning standards, I have always done and showed the best of me. I avoided failures and just wanted to have a good presentable record. I have not tried getting zero or making the worst actions inside the school premise. I have been a good student. My classmates before and my sisters could attest to that. I just really feel very blessed to acquire the gift of knowledge even if my parents were not able to instill and pass intelligence to me, also knowing that my father is not smart. At home, my family would even make a joke that good thing, I did not inherit the brain of my father. My father would simply laugh and add that I am his hope that he knows I could make it. In return, I laughed as well but said that my father is smart in other ways, and I am very sure of that. He immediately hugged me after hearing it and said that I am his most favorite son. Well, who could not be called a favorite son, knowing that I am his only one son? What I did in order to hone my knowledge more is to listen well to my teachers in school, and I read a lot of books, as well. Things went pretty well, that time. I felt so happy to be able to finish the standards asked of us.

I was 11 years old when this picture was taken.

One sunny morning, my father and mother asked us some random questions while we were on the farm, staring at the animals eating grasses. One question that hit me the most was when they asked me what I would like to become in the future. They asked me if I want to follow the footsteps of my uncles to go overseas and earn a lot of money, or follow the other uncle who became a school principal and earn good memories with kids, or maybe I could become an engineer and build a good building, a pilot and travel the world, or any dream I like. When they asked me that, it seemed that the world stopped. I questioned myself about what I really wanted. I answered my parents that I still need to ponder about it. Minutes after, they hugged me and said that I can be who I want to be if I just trust the very self that I could do it, and if I work hard. They told me they could not send me to a great school, and I know it since we do not have money, so I just answered that I will work hard for it and take risks. But minutes later, my mother approached me. She said she knew what I like and so I asked her. My mother knew I want to become a doctor. She narrated the experience I had before when I was young. She could still remember the time we went to the clinic and the time when I saw a doctor there. She also described the exact reaction I had when the doctor started checking on me. My mother could also not forget the questions I raised while we were going home. She then hugged me and said, I could be a doctor if I will work hard for it. I could be anyone, a better person, a professional person, and a person who is brave enough to face struggles in life. Right there and then, I smiled at her and hugged her back. My mother really knew what's best for her children.

Years passed by, a lot of moments already happened. My elder sisters got married. They were not able to reach their dreams. They married early. My sisters lived a simple life, as well, just like my father and mother. They now lived far away from us, together with their in-laws. My parents still checked on their whereabouts and supported them in all that they could. I know my parents somewhat felt sad, but

I guess they just respected my elder sisters' decision. Well, that's what parents usually do, just being always there to support their children no matter what, for as long as the situation they are in would not cause them harm. That was the time I said to myself I have to make my parents proud and seek my own fortune. I should not get married early. I have not helped my family yet. Whenever I get married in the future, I have to be equipped and ready— financially, emotionally, and mentally. So, after a few years of schooling, I realized that I really wanted to be a doctor. I did not want to be a teacher, just like my uncle. I did not also want to be an engineer or a policeman. I only wanted to become a doctor. There was one time, when I was still six years old, which my mother narrated, that was the time when my mother brought me to the clinic meters away from home. It was just a small clinic in town. A doctor came to the clinic to visit everyone working there. He was wearing very clean and attractive clothing, with a stethoscope on his neck. I immediately said, WOW. He came nearer to me and asked if I was fine. My mother said to him that I was sick, that I got a fever. So, the doctor checked on me and prescribed medicines to take and gave advice for me not to possibly get sick again. He was very gentle and caring. Because of that situation, I immediately told myself that I want to be like him someday. I want to care for the sick. I want to help people heal. I want to save lives. While going home, I asked my mother if it is hard to be like him. She responded that it is going to take several years to become one. Things will never get easy, but success will surely come. She also added that the path to being a doctor is very expensive. Upon hearing it, I felt the excitement, but at the same time, I felt sad. Excitement because I want to become a doctor someday and a bit sad because my dream somewhat caused me to feel down, most especially when my mother said it is very expensive to become a doctor. But being a doctor never disappeared in my mind, every time I see pictures in the school of nurses and doctors, I felt energized. I said to myself that no matter how difficult it could be, I'll give it a try.

This was taken when I was 14 years old.

Going back to the time I finished schooling after a few years, I thought to make my dream into a reality. I told my parents that I want to become a doctor. When they heard me saying that, they never said NO; instead, full of encouragement was given to me. My parents said that if I really like that career, then I should go for it. They added that they could hardly support me financially if I get through it, but father assured me that he would beg for his brothers to support me and look for ways that are within his capacities. My mother, on the other hand, said I can make it. She believed I can be like the doctor we saw in the clinic years ago when I was still young. She knew from that situation that I wanted to become like him. Still, she was just observant and quiet, because she also knew that kids' dreams change over time, most especially when they see something new and interesting. With the words I have listened to, my soul was given more life. Because of these things, I attempted to take a pre-medical test. Taking it was never easy. There are lots of hurdles to encounter. Since the CASTE system in India is followed and observed in all medical colleges, and there's a limited number for students in medicine in all colleges, I said to myself I need to take things very seriously. I needed to be part of the top list. I have to be part of it. I have to work hard for it. Since the test was administered a month or two after I inquired, I was happy because I still have time to study and give it all. I still had 45 days to nail it. Imagine, for 45 days, I did not go out of my room. It consumed me a month and a few days. I just stayed there, no going out. I had to burn the midnight oil every night. I had to review a lot. I kept studying only chemistry, microbiology, and biology since these are the main focus of being a doctor. I did pretty well during the review. My parents supported me. They just knocked on the door to give me food. I was all alone in the room. No distractions. No noise. I was very serious at that time. I did not have any time to talk with other family members. Still, they understood the situation, and they supported me all the way. Books and reviewers were my only companion. My uncle, who is a school principal, lend me books from school and from colleagues, so I could study better. It was not a piece of cake. It was also tiring, and there were times I felt drained. There was even a time I fell asleep and even had a dream that I am still studying. Even in my dreams, I was still studying. Funny right, but I think it's normal. Maybe I was so engrossed about studying that time. The 45 days were filled with studying and studying and studying. The only day that I decided to come out was the test date. Yes, you heard it right, because I did not want to waste time. I did not want to fail. I did not want to take another course aside from being a doctor. I did not want my family to feel sad, especially my parents. That was my greatest dream. Unluckily, things did not turn as what I worked for and as what I expected. I did not make it. I did not get into medicine. Instead, I was qualified for dental. However, I had no interest in dental. That was not my dream. I felt sad to be very honest. Tears even fell down from my eyes. I came home, looking sad. My parents asked me why and so I narrated things to them and how the exam was like. I mentioned things I did not know. When my parents knew about it, they talked with me in private. They hugged me directly. They comforted me and said, life does not end there, that my and our dreams are bigger than it. There will always be next time. Maybe it was really not for me. Maybe it is not my destiny. Maybe being a doctor is for someone else. Maybe I am for another path. A path that is way better than being a doctor. A path that could make me happier and make myself and our family prosper. Honestly, I felt down, but seeing my parents like that, uplifting my interest and my choices, somewhat gave me a wake-up call that I have to keep going. I have to try and try and try again until I could reach all my dreams in life.

Chapter III

A Journey to the Big City

When you come from a rural area, the notion and perspective of an urban place is really something different compared to what you are accustomed to. Sometimes, it is frightening to imagine, but sometimes, it could be high time to explore more opportunities in order to bring something helpful to where you came from and also to reach your dreams, despite all the possible fears you have in mind. It takes guts and courage to be in a place that you have never been to years back.

Cities have been considered as great sources of knowledge, culture, and also, social life. In cities, you could find vibrant cultures. A large population can also be found. Rich social opportunities are also offered in the cities.

People who live in the city have better transport facilities compared to those who are living in the village. There are so many facilities. There is telecommunication. There is communication. There is a highway. There is electricity. People get to lead a comfortable and more natural way of life. More opportunities for earning money can also be found in the city. Children who were born in such a place can get a better education than those living in small towns because there are better schools to choose from. There are also more places for entertainment, and there are lots of things to be done when you prefer to have a city life. There are more chances for employment. Jobs that are of greater range and jobs that are of higher pay. Living standards are higher in cities. It is easier and faster to earn more money. In the province, it is mostly agriculture-based. People depend on agriculture to make money and to have food. In the city, you can simply find a job in the call center, in factories, and in other establishments. Internet, schools, universities, industries, hospitals, roads, factories, airports, railway stations, telephone, and facilities of gas are available.

Since I have lots of dreams in life, for myself and for my family, and I did not want to end my future to be at stake, just like what my father has, I moved to a bigger city with my cousins who were pharmacists. I thought of it many times and had to gather great courage for myself. I told myself that I can do it. I should not allow my dreams to just be buried meters in the soil. I asked permission from my parents, and they allowed me to. At first, they were hesitant because I was still a teenager at that time. My mother was worried, so as my father. They were afraid if I could do it. It would be far from home, and they could not look after me there, but I assured them that I can do it; anyway, my cousins would be there too. I explained to them that I have to do it for myself and for them. I could not just settle looking for my dreams in the town where I live. I have to look for opportunities. I have to look for other chances. I needed to open my own door of opportunities. I was just thankful because my parents permitted me to. They just advised me to take extra care of myself. They warned me that living in the city would not be easy. Every move requires money. Nothing is free. And so, I took risks.

I have to work hard for it, no matter where I could reach just to reach it. With that, I chose to do IELTS to be able to go overseas, since it is one of the requirements in going to other countries and working there, and hoping that someday, I could also have the life that my two uncles are living. When I was young, I could see the big difference in the life of my father and the life of my uncles. Working overseas somewhat gave me an idea before that I could get rich by doing the same. And so, when I did IELTS, I started some sort of training and coaching. It was not easy, I tell you. It was complex. It was tricky. But I was able to make it. Nonetheless, I encountered this new but big problem. I did not know how to make a passport. I was already very excited when I finished IELTS but did not expect I have to process for my passport. Because I did not know anything about it, I used an agent to make a passport. He was the one doing all the processing, and I just paid him. I thought it will be given to me real quick, but I was wrong. I waited for days and months, but I was not able to get my passport until it reached for one year, and with all honesty, I was quite stressed and really anxious. I even thought of another way if I could not make it. Days after that, finally, I got it. I now have a passport. I can now go overseas and look for a greener pasture.

For me, real-life and the real world started in the city where I moved because I was only 16 at that time when I moved to a bigger city. It took me lots of guts to do that. Imagine what a 16- year-old boy can do in a city in which he did not even know what to expect from it. The scope is very far from home, really far. The surroundings are exactly the opposite of what's in our town. Farms are absent, animals can't be seen, people do now walk on foot all the time, they preferred riding in cars or buses, food is different, and everybody seems to be very busy day by day. You have to move fast and fast and fast. What's with me is my dream and one photo of my family. Yes, I brought one photo which has my mother, my father, and my elder sisters. I know it would take a long period of time before I could get back to the place where I was born and to be with my family again. Even if I am a man, I also how to miss my loved ones. When I arrived in the city, my knowledge is limited yet. My cousins were there to orient me with things. I did not know everything under the sun. Really, I felt like I was incapable of doing other things in the city because of little or lack of knowledge. I did not know how to ride on the train. I did not know how to access the internet. I did not know how to get food in an automated machine. I did not know even google, because of the fact that I only came from a small village, far from civilization. I did not even know to use a computer, because we did not have computers in school before, not even in our house. I was like having a culture shock. Everything was new to me. Everything was out of my grasp. Everything was not part of my part life. My parents were correct. Being in the city is challenging. Almost everything is also run by money. Without money, you can't move, you can't buy, you can't access things, and you can't get what you want. However, I gained good friends who helped me adjust to city life, aside from my cousins. By the way, my cousin, who is a pharmacist, already applied for a job in pharmaceutical businesses and got hired. Because I needed to make an income, I looked for possible jobs that would fit my qualifications. I went job hunting. It was hard. It was tough to look for a job in a city. There are many competitors that you have to pass through. Nonetheless, when I asked suggestions from a few people about what job to take, some of them in the city advised me that I can work in a call center for part-time because it was already the trend. Many BPO companies were already building their names in the city, so I said I would try. Money was really a problem, and there was no money coming home monthly. I should have work. I can't just depend on the help given by my cousins. How would you expect me to live if I will not work? So, I took another risk. I applied to a call center, and fortunately, I got hired. I made my own money by working. I started working in a call center, following the night shift. Good thing I had a good grasp of the English language years back. I was able to use what I have learned in school now. Right there and then, I earned minimum wage monthly, just enough to support my daily needs. It was my very first time to earn something for myself, and I felt good with it. The feeling of fulfillment is really different when you get to receive your salary for the very first time. It was out of hard work. However, I met some difficulties while working. Well, at first, I found it hard since I was into the night shift. I needed to work at night. My body clock was not used to that, I easily felt tired and sleepy, but a good thing, as days passed by, I was already used to it. I was able to get an adjustment with my time. Since my earnings are not enough, I even looked for another source of income and another way to keep myself busy and for me to grow more in knowledge and experience. I asked a few friends another possible job to land. Then, they suggested me to do this. In the morning, I went to an English language training center and also got a chance to teach a few things there. I was able to share my knowledge with others, most especially to those who were like me before, full of innocence, but wrapped with goals in life. I was able to meet a lot of people. I was able to know as well that they came from different places. They also took risks, just like me. So far, everything went well. I also earned a little money while working there. I did the same routine every day, working at night in the call center and in the morning, going to the English Language Training to teach. I was just really fortunate that despite me, being a freshman to the said city, I was able to easily cope up with it. It was kind of stressful and exhausting because I only have a few hours left for sleeping, but in my mind, I was full of motivation. I was motivated to do it to be able to save money, as well. I needed to have savings so that I could study. I still had a dream at that time, to get a degree.

I was 19 years old when this photo was taken.

In February 2009, I took another risk once more. My life has been filled with risks, but there was never a time I regretted any of them. You know, I have to take another journey to have a better life. I still have my dreams. I also want to study. I did not wish that my life will just revolve between the call canter and the English Language Training. I dreamt of more. Good thing, my parents also taught me how to become independent. During the times that I missed them, I just always glanced at the family picture that we had, hoping that it would ease the longing that I felt. It was not easy to be far from home, to be far from family. At least during these times, I was able to stand on my own and to do what I wanted for myself and for my family back home. And so, I moved to another country and applied for a study visa. I have learned from others that bigger opportunities come to those who could get a degree in New Zealand.

People also said that job hiring is great in the country. I came from India, so if I could go to New Zealand, then that is something to be very proud of.

What's good with New Zealand? Why did I think of going there? Well, these are my reasons. This country is 11, 963 kilometers away from India. It is very famous in the whole world for its incredible scenery. It is also one of the safest and one of the most beautiful. You can find ranging from sweeping mountains to vast underground cave systems in New Zealand. There are also gigantic glaciers, boiling hot springs, rugged coastline, and golden-sand beaches in the said country. Expect as well for cool cities, wonderful wildlife, hidden spots, and a lot more. There are just so many places to visit and various things to do in New Zealand. In terms of education, New Zealand is renowned for being among the top 20 OECD countries for good quality education. I learned this when I searched about it before, and it has been evident until now. The country offers excellent study opportunities and world- class education. No wonder why it has become one of the most attractive destinations for international students and aspirants. Students preferred to study and live in New Zealand because of its low cost of living and good exclusive facilities. Universities in the country are considered to be giving the best education with affordable fees. Many Indian students, like me, chose New Zealand due to its annual tuition fees. The living expenses, as I said earlier, are cheaper compared to another study abroad like UK, USA, or Canada. The British Education Model became the basis of education in the country. Because of these, I desired to be in New Zealand and be able to study there.

It would be a new beginning for me, and maybe, New Zealand is the answer to my dreams. It could be the key to my goals. I could start a new beginning in New Zealand. I could make my dreams to a reality, in the said country. But things were also not that easy. To be able to go to New Zealand, many hurdles have to be successfully encountered. One big problem I met was money. Yes, it was money again. My savings were not enough. My money was only enough for a plane ticket. If only I had lots of money. But I guess it really had to be that way because if not, I couldn't have worked harder. Going back to the story, I needed to show money for the purpose of financial stability. That is always the rule of other countries. Show money serves as evidence of funds to support my study. In New Zealand, if you wish to study there, a student must provide evidence to show that he or she has enough money to support himself or herself while studying in the country. You need to have show money. Now that became my other problem. The problem with where to get show money.

My parents back in India did not have enough. As I said, my savings were also not enough. Because of this, I had to beg my uncles to sponsor me. I found ways to contact them. I called them one by one. They were only the close people I know who could lend me some money, and my parents did not have much money, right from the very beginning. I begged to them because I was so desperate to take another opportunity in life. Good thing that my uncles helped me. I assured them that their money would not be put into waste. I know how hard it is for them to work far from home and far from family. I will study hard in New Zealand to be able to get a good and stable job. Also, I told them that soon, I could repay them for the good things that they have done for my family and for me. What's another brighter side of the situation was this, the dollar value that time was still cheap. The dollar value was not so high that time and very minimal fees were charged to me. Finally, the long wait is over.

I traveled 15-16 hours just to reach the country. I was all alone. During the whole duration of the travel, I kept on writing on my notebook my plans, so I could have a guide, and I will never forget. I stared again at our family picture, and I talked with each of my family through the photo I brought from home. These were the exact words I said that time. "To you, my dearest father and mother, when I become successful, you need not dig the soil again. You need not exert so much sweat just to give us food. You need not work very early and stop working very late. You will be resting and taking a vacation in lieu of the times you worked day and night for us. To my mother, we could have your dreamland soon. We could build a house for the family. You will no longer need to repeatedly use ingredients and put little by little every time you cook meals, you can already cook anything you like with all the fresh raw ingredients you could ask for, soon.

You need not work day and night anymore, just like what my parents did. To my sisters, your children will surely have a good quality of education. I will help you all. I can surely do this. Wish me luck! We will help each other to have a good life. "This time was so emotional for me. I was speaking to them through the picture only. Tears fell down from my eyes again. How I missed them so much. Memories of childhood just kept bringing back in my mind.

A few hours later, I was able to arrive in New Zealand safely through a plane. I traveled 15-16 hours just to reach the country. I was all alone. I only had a big backpack with all my clothes inside. When I first stepped out of the plane, I immediately expressed a big W-O-W. It was my first time in New Zealand, and I have already been in love and in awe with its beauty the moment I arrived. The landscape is so green, and I could say it's where I have only seen the bluest skies. Everything is very clean. What they say about New Zealand being very serious about conservation, clean, and sustainable living is definitely true. The country is just simply amazing and wonderful. Beautiful sceneries can be found, breathtaking views, and good people or shall I say, good New Zealanders/ good Kiwis. Everywhere I look, the people seemed to be very friendly. They gave me a smile, even if they did not know me. Talking about the climate, good thing, it is somewhat the same as the climate in India. I need not adjust a lot. I directly took a rest after I arrived and thought of the things I have to do first. My excitement was just so immeasurable at that time. I could not contain my happiness, too. Imagine, this was just a dream before, which is to go overseas. Now, I am here. I know, I am still far from reality, but at least I have already taken steps for it. In my mind, I've got so many plans that have to be put into action. I needed to pursue my education. I needed to get part-time jobs for me to be able to provide for my very own needs and pay for my own bills. I told myself I will, and I can do multiple jobs while studying. I could also work day and night, just like my father. There is and will never be a room for giving up. That time, I already felt shy and did not want to ask help from my uncles anymore. They have already given a lot. They, too, have their families to feed and children to support. I kept on telling myself that I should not fail my family. That I will only come home when I already have money and have attained something. Right there and then, I started looking for brighter opportunities. I researched a lot, studied the rules and regulations of New Zealand so I could not violate any law. I also started roaming around to be acquainted with the streets and every corner. I had to do it. I had to familiarize my surroundings. Since my main purpose in coming here is to study, I already thought of what degree to take. I looked for many universities and found one that would fit me. I wanted a Bachelor's Degree, that is what I have been saying back then, but only a Diploma in Science and technology is available. Well, I still took risks. I did my best to make friends at the university I was in. I am just very thankful because everyone seemed to be very helpful and assistive to me. They always assisted me, most especially during my first few days. I had no idea which room to go, who would be my professors, which way I should go next, and all that stuff. However, I was able to slowly adjust and get along with things. My cousins used to contact me and asked if I was doing well. I immediately responded that I was taking everything in moderation--- slowly adjusting with food, with people, and with the entirely new environment I am in. Oh, how I missed them, and I also missed home. I missed my father, my father, my sisters, my uncles, my grandparents, and my aunts. I missed everyone back home, but I have to be emotionally strong. I needed to focus on the very reason why I'm in New Zealand.

Chapter IV

A New Life in New Zealand

Colin Powell, a former United States Defense Secretary, once said, "A dream does not become a reality through magic; it takes sweat, determination, and hard work." This quote is very relatable to the experiences that I had to go through when I first came and take a journey to New Zealand. The word, "hard work," speaks about everything I had to go through just to get the life I have now.

My life in New Zealand started in the year 2009. I came in and took a Diploma in Science and technology. I came in, and then you know, tried to mingle and be like others. I was quite a smart kid from the start, but initially, a few days after were different. I came in, and people said to me why not choose business studies because they usually get a commission from those colleges and stuff like that. They suggested that, but I did pretty well in the course I took. After one month, during one of my classes, I guess it was Microbiology class with our Professor Francis; there was one email that dropped in into her account, which said that they are looking for a student graduate. They are looking for a graduate of microbiology, so I immediately said to my professor that I need to go out to go to the toilet. Well, that was just an excuse. So, I went out and immediately, I called the same number. It was from Jackie. I remembered Jackie. Since the school's phones are high tech phones, I called her and asked about the

39

email she sent, and I told her that I want to work for her and that I can be trusted. In my mind, I kept on saying to myself that I need to get this job in order to earn money, and in order to pay for my expenses. So the next morning, I went for the interview. Immediately, I went for it. Then, she has sort of hiring me. My heart was filled with glee. It was my very first job in New Zealand. I promised Jackie that I would do well, and she would not regret choosing me over the others. By the time other students rank her, the next day, I already had a job. She already hired me. And then, I kept on working, and I kept on studying, at the same time. However, what I earned is not enough. I still had to look for another source of income. I looked around and saw signage from a restaurant looking for a waiter. The wage is not that big, as well, but it's going to be a simple and easy job. Anyway, it was just part-time. And so, I started working in a restaurant doing as a waiter. Things like that. I earned, but still, not enough to sustain my needs, so I inquired in McDonald's. Good thing they are still looking for a male server. And so, I also started working in

McDonald's. Then, I realized I needed money in preparation for my fees in school. And so, I started working in Pizza Hut. I also worked in dominos. I worked as a delivery driver. But the thing is, I kept working with Jackie as well as a food technician. But I knew, and I believed, they would not have much time for me in terms of the hours, so I started training myself in the production. Because obviously, knowing about my residence in New Zealand, I needed a skilled job. I knew as a laboratory technician, they only had fifteen to twenty hours, so I told Jackie if I could look and help in the production if she could train me. So, I started training. They used to do a kiwi fruit powder for nutraceuticals supplements . Then, they use millet. They used to make a powder out of it. Because of the training I acquired, I started working in the production. Everything went pretty well, but then, the moment I was about to finish my course, I got a job interview at Xtend-Life, and that company used to make supplements. Yes, you heard it right. They make dietary supplements. I was one and a half year in my course. Still, it was actually hard because one year of it was paid when I came from India, but the next six months, I had to pay it on my own, so I borrowed here from a few good friends; cousin brother in Sydney and stuff, and then, I paid the fee. So during the last day, I had an exam and then, at that time I was invited to the interview. I said okay, that's definitely fine but then obviously I had applied for so many jobs when I was working with Jackie because in my free time I used to apply for the jobs, different jobs, so to speak. Then the woman I walk through the interview asked which CV they should take on board because one says there's a pursuing course and one says already pursued. She asked me which one is great. So I said, I've been honest with them because I have been a smart kid since then and because I will not let any job to just pass through me without me getting it and doing my best. So, I started applying for jobs by saying them I am already qualified six months before. Even if I did not finish the job, but then I knew that I will not get the job. Then, they had some, one CV which obviously says I have finished studies while the other one says I have not finished yet, so I said to them that I already completed it. Finally, I got the job, so which was pretty good. I was very happy at that time. I have never failed during the interview. Even if I am not that good in the English language, still, I was able to nail it. Right there and then, I started working. The company is used to make some supplements, so my job is to make sure that the quality test is done well with the raw materials in the lab and stuff. I did not know anything. I did not know how to write an e-mail. I was pretty poor in English. I carried on. I still worked. I observed a lot with how others work, so I get acquainted with things. Also, I got good training, too. But in the evening, instead of taking a rest and doing school stuff, I used to work for an Indian Restaurant. The restaurant I was able to work with offers mouth-watering dishes to all customers. The restaurant was very classy, and also, food prices are manageable. When I worked there, I brought with me the proper etiquette taught by my mother and father at home. Sometimes, I received tips coming from customers, for they liked my services. The owner of the restaurant would also commend me for my performance. My meal is also free in the evening in the restaurant, so instead of buying something to eat, I just saved that portion of money into my piggy bank. Despite being tired and busy at work, things still work pretty well for me because I used to go to the gym in the morning, have swimming, go to

Work, go to school, and in the evening, go to the restaurant again and work. Sometimes at the weekend, I also used to drive a taxi, and at the weekend, I used to work in McDonald's. So basically, for long seven days, I used to work, work, and work. I would say the seven days are very long to finish because day by day, I had not time to rest. Days were purely for work and studies. Just purely moving day and night. That carried on for roughly around one and a half years. Imagine, it took me more than 400-500 days to do that. That happened roughly June 2010 until roughly around June 2012. I used to do three jobs. At 5:00 o'clock in the morning until 2:00 o'clock at the weekends, I work in McDonald's. And then, 8:00 o'clock in the morning until 5:00 in the office, and then 5:00 o'clock to 11 o'clock in the restaurant. It was like a merry-go-round set-up. So everything went well. I was making a lot of money. That was my purpose of doing multiple jobs, of being able to acquire a lot of money. I was able to secure my residence in New Zealand. Then, I was able to buy a taxi business, so I started doing a taxi. Imagine, I worked in McDonald's at 5:00 o'clock in the morning until 2:00 o'clock in the weekends, 8:00 o'clock in the morning until 5:00 in the office, and then 5:00 o'clock to 11 o'clock in the restaurant, then Thursday, Friday, Saturday, Sunday, I used to drive a taxi as well. Oh, my God. Reminiscing now, I could feel that I was so drained and stressed at that time. I worked 24/7. I was super busy. I was like McDonald's, opening and functioning for 24 hours with no rest and with no day-off. And all that happened. Obviously, I made money. Because I already earned a lot, I decided to buy a car. Remember when I told you earlier that I want to own a car so I need not to walk and walk and walk? Yes, I was able to acquire one, and I felt like I am starting to get the things that I want for myself and for my family. That moment,

I already contacted my cousins and shared with them that I was able to get a car already. They shouted with glee and said, W-O-W. They asked me how I was able to do it. I said to them that I embraced multiple jobs. They were shocked, but at the same time, they felt worried. They told me I have to take good care of myself. After all, my health is still my greatest wealth. My cousins knew how eager I am in terms of things, and they also know what my dreams are. I positively assured them that I would take extra precautions about my health, that I would take good care of myself, and that I will not break my promise to them. A few days after, I also started planning to build a house in India. Things like that.

I was already in New Zealand at this time when I was 21 years old.

I also came back to India for the very first time, after I got my New Zealand residence visa. When I came home, my parents directly hugged me, and they cried. It was like a family reunion. They were so happy seeing me again, after how many months of no contact with each other. My mother approached me and said these exact words, "I have been praying for your safety, my son. We were worried about you. It pained us, most especially me, your mom, to not be able to take care of you. I know how hard it could have been for you that you are far from us. Finally, we are together again. Look at yourself, you have changed a lot now. You have left with so much innocence in your mind but filled with so many dreams and goals in your life. I am very proud of you, my son. You have a difference in your life. Keep it up, Gaurav." Tears continued to fall down from my mother's eyes. After my mother, I tapped the back of my father. The moment I did

it, he unconsciously cried. He said to me these, "Thank you for working hard. I know, you have exerted so much determination, eagerness, and patience with the things that you did in New Zealand. The moment you were able to reach that country, I was already proud. This tie that you had come home and visit us, you made me prouder. Thank you because you learned from my mistakes in the past. Thank you for pouring to the family the things that I lack. Lastly, thank you, my son, for working hard for us. You did use our present situation as your greatest motivation. Keep doing it, my son." When I heard these words, the hardships and the pain I felt while working hard in New Zealand seemed to be healed. I knew my decisions were right. I was happy because they appreciated my own sacrifices for the family. I immediately narrated to them the different jobs I went through in New Zealand, and they were shocked. They were sad and worried because what if my health would ask for a break, but I was lucky that my whole body cooperated. I remained healthy despite losing weight. I was also able to visit my sisters. I brought food for them and other stuff for their children. I could feel how happy they were when they saw me. One of my sisters said she could not believe such things happening. She could not believe that a petite boy, referring to me when I was young, would be a grown-up man, now and slowly reaching many dreams in life. They were very happy, and I was happy, too. I hugged my nieces and whispered in their ears that they should study hard. I would help them all the way until they could finish their studies. Because of the money I saved, I was able to transfer a lot of money back home and was able to buy land. My father was with me when I bought it. I told him that the land is not for me, but for them. I promised them that I would build them a house soon when I could already find another way to make a higher income. My father thanked and said that I already made a good start and that there's nothing to rush with things. He advised me to keep going for the perfect time will come to me. I believed what he told me. So, I invested my money in the land. Obviously, my family and my uncles were very glad because they did not expect and know that I would climb that fast. My uncle, who is a school principal, told me that he's very proud of me, too. He knew then that I can go far way better than my father and my sisters because he believed in my potential, just like my teachers before. My other uncles, who are in Austria, also heard about my whereabouts and were also happy because the help that they gave me was not wasted and that I made true of my promise to them. Things like that happened, and it carried on.

Chapter V

My highest Realization

Days passed by, I went back to New Zealand. My family was sad because I had to leave them again, but I told them I had to do it because my dreams are still alive and kicking. I am still blessed because ever since they were much supportive. They wished me luck and continued praying for my safety. They could not wait for the time we could be reunited once more. As I came back to New Zealand, it was time for me to leave Extend Life, and so I asked myself. Do I really want this to happen in my entire life? Do I really want to spend all my hours working with my multiple jobs? Do I want this same set-up to happen? Should I work again in McDonald's at 5:00 o'clock in the morning until 2:00 o'clock at the weekends, 8:00 o'clock in the morning until 5:00 in the office, and then 5:00 o'clock to 11 o'clock in the restaurant, then Thursday, Friday, Saturday, Sunday, drive a taxi again? And the answer was a big NO. It is not that I did not want those jobs, those jobs helped me. Those jobs fed me. Those jobs paid for my residence. Those jobs allowed me to buy land. Those jobs sustained me, but I dreamt for more, and I can't just consume my whole life doing such. I believed something is waiting for me from afar, and I am referring to the word SUCCESS. That part of the time, I already knew the dietary supplement industry, which I learned from my training and experiences in Xtend-Life. I already knew the game in terms of how to make the tablet capsules, how to handle the raw materials, and how to import the raw materials. The full picture of doing everything is on my brain, starting from what I should do first, what I should do next, and what should I expect to happen or what is my expected result. I learned it over one and a half years. I have spoken to people. I have always been a curious guy. Everything I touched even if I was not in control in the process, I knew what was going on. As I said earlier, I also made a series of observations. I was very observant of things. And then, after three months, as I said, I left Extend Life. My boss felt sad. He knew how passionate I was when I worked in his company. Many people would even commend him for hiring me. People would say I have contributed a lot to my boss' business. In my part, I was also kind of hurt and sad because I have spent almost two good years there, and I have built good memories already, but I realized that I should not waste time. I must move on. Life should be like that, full of moving on and working hard again. Right there and then, I thought of starting my own company, why not? I know it was a very big risk to start one, but I never felt afraid of doing it. I will give it a try. Anyway, there are a lot of trading companies in India, who would be exporting the products to New Zealand, so why can't I do it. I could make bigger money with this plan. And the thing is, I am the only son who will look after my parents. I needed to give them a good life, knowing that they are not getting any younger. As I narrated minutes ago, my sisters are already married. I still need to provide them a good house. I still wanted them to savor a good life. As much as I can, I will work hard for them. So, I planned things very well. There should never be a single error for this risk I am going to take. I planned everything and made sure I could get a high percentage of success for this. I really thought of it as a business that involves traveling between India and New Zealand. That would be very ideal, and that sort of happened because from Xtend-Life, I went on several meetings and met good people with extraordinary experiences, who also started businesses. Then they want to expand to New Zealand, and I said why not. So, I reached out to those people. I talked to them and asked for help and made some negotiations. Since they already knew me, it was not hard for them to trust me. They considered me a good partner and, at the same time, an ideal friend.

Immediately after I left Xtend-Life, I did another significant thing. I started doing a study, and the study is about Bachelor of Medical Imaging. It was very, very hard to get selected into that because there are only three institutions here in New Zealand and three Polytechnics that offer such courses, and they only take 35 students for it per year. Hence, it was really a huge competition for that course. It was very challenging. Despite the fact that I was already processing for the business at that time, I still did not forget my quest for education. I think it's truly a good course because any person could get to work as a Medical Radiation Technologist. So, that course kept going. I was into it. I started the first year and second year, all clear. My records were good. I still had a good academic performance. My professors were still in awe of my determination and eagerness to learn. While in my third year, I started my business and brand to run. Just like before, I am now back on track in doing multiple things at the same time. My business and my brand are called Botanic Health Care. The name was chosen, keeping in mind that we can sell the raw materials and we can sell the finished product. I was so happy to launch it in India. My parents were very happy too, so as my siblings, my uncles, my aunts, and my cousins. At first, I was just hoping that it would turn out good, but yes, the business boomed as days passed by. That thing carried on. By that time, my business was doing very well. My whole the family was very proud. The way of living of my family started to change. My life started to change, as well. I could even make up to 300,000 dollars a year. It was a very big money. Going back to my studies, I thought if I really want to practice being a Medical Radiation Technologist, because to be able to practice such, I need to achieve 180 hours a year. With me, I have been traveling back to India again and again. It was not possible to achieve the 180 hours asked of me. Months after, I finished my Bachelor in Medical Imaging. It was almost done, but I did not do technical for six months, which was the final step because I was too overloaded. That was just too much. I run a taxi business, I ran a business in India. I also study. It was really too much for me. I also do work on

Zealand Immigration Ltd as in-charge of Immigration law papers. I used to provide consulting and manage their work visa and residence visa to New Zealand residents.

This is the Zealand Immigration Ltd.

As soon as I left Medical Imaging, I started this small office on consulting and started this Zealand Immigrating Ltd. If I would go for it, I am afraid I need to sacrifice my business, and I can't do that. My business brought food to my loved ones. Then, I asked myself if I really want to do my path in being a Medical Radiation Technologist. I thought of it many times. I considered the possible pros and cons. And so, I said to myself that I am not going to move further with that. So, it was just put behind, and then I was too focused on the Botanic Healthcare business. It was doing very well. I could not believe that it prospered that much. Before, my business was just a beginner, but now, it was able to reach other countries, and many people liked it. Others did not just like my products, they loved it. They kept on coming back to buy and patronize us. Because of that, I was able to produce other businesses. I was able to invest in other fields, which brought money to me, as well. As of today, for eight years now, we have exported up to 75 countries a lot of our products. All that has happened. And then, obviously, it carried on making money. I handled my money very well. I am not the type of person who always tends to become a "one-day millionaire." I always planned what to spend. I listed everything. I also ensured I have so many savings in my bank account. I made sure every money I have was well-spent. We have tried nothingness before, so I know how it felt to have no money to get in times of difficult times. But, I was never thrifty when it comes to family. Whenever they needed money, I give. Whenever a relative gets sick, I helped. Whenever a niece wants to study, I supported it. These things I do, selflessly, for the love of my family.

Moving further, I have always been doing hard work in everything that I do because obviously, we were not rich. Back then, we needed to work in order to have something to eat. My parents sacrificed a lot on the farm. My father was not able to finish schooling, and you know that already. I mean, the three of us, me and my sisters, we used to finish school whether it is summer or it is winter. We experienced any of it. We come home, we drink a lot of water because we walked from very far away. Good thing we were not used to coughing and colds. Maybe, our immune system was already strong because our body is already used with summer and winter, even at a young age. And then, going home, we would help our parents with the cows, goats, and etc. And then, we also get some manure and other stuff. Those were the memories with my dad and my mom. Obviously, with my sisters. We were trained to help them and do the chores before we get to do our home works and eats dinner. About our animals, we usually buy goats, and then we chose the smaller ones, they are called the baby goats, and then, we will raise them up. Then, we just sell them off when they are big already in order to make some money, so we can pay our school fee, and we can pay our expenses. It somewhat became a cycle for years. So definitely, everything we had before was hard years. Those years became my daily reflection. I could not afford to see my parents do the same routine until they get old and leave them with no choice. I wanted them to be out of that scenario. That is why I worked very, very, very hard. Every work I've been through was very tiring. It was really difficult. I even started having malnutrition, and I started losing my hair because of stress in doing the night shift before in the call center. I could still remember that stress and hair loss became the exchange of the minimum wage I received in the call center I worked with. I could hardly take a night of good sleep at that time since I also worked another job. Other struggles were in McDonald's, the Indian Restaurant, my work as a delivery boy, my work as a taxi driver, and all the other kinds of work I had, but that's fine. Everything I did was fine. It was truly a hard time, but I was able to get through with those hardships. In life, it is normal to sacrifice a lot in order to yield better results in the end. As they always say, when there is no pain, there will always be no gain. Well, that was a good reflection of my past experiences, which I will surely cherish for the rest of my life.

In terms of major events in my life, obviously, these include schooling, getting jobs, starting my businesses. Then during my Medical Studies, I started studying Immigration business. Yes, I never stopped learning. I was very open-minded with other things and very welcoming to other opportunities. Everything was going side by side. I already get used to doing many things at the same time. I seemed to be like an octopus, which has lots of tentacles in it. Despite having lots of things to attend to, I made sure each of the things I do, I give passion and commitment. I did everything with hard work. So, that time. I did things altogether. I was doing Botanic Healthcare. I was doing training with the Immigration business because I got a license as an immigration adviser. I was also doing my taxi business. My taxi business has been with me through the years. I never left it because it also brought me a high income. Taxi is very helpful as one of the sources of transportation here in New Zealand, so it is very in demand. It was very hard work. A lot of hard work, if you, yourself, could sum it all. All that carried on, and then I thought about to just starting my immigration business because I already got a license as an immigration adviser, so I started it. It was really a new opportunity for me. I learned about it because one of my partners in one of my businesses suggested it to me since he is doing it himself. He told me it is good business. It would be very in-demand since many are immigrants here in New Zealand. Settlers just simply come and go. So, it would definitely take a good click. But before I started it, again, just like the usual, I planned things very well. I had my plans arranged in order and then made sure to choose good people. I also had possible solutions in mind whenever I could encounter problems with the immigration business. This is also what I usually do with my businesses, even with those that already started. I am already packed with alternatives and solutions, so whenever problems may arise, then, my team and I are already ready with it. Since it's a new business for me, I also had to look for the perfect people. I am referring to the word "perfect" with those who are hardworking. So, I started looking for the rights ones. Days passed by, I was able to find a few good individuals. However, I still needed someone who could be a great partner. Obviously, I was looking for somebody who could help me run it and then, there I met a fine-looking woman, who then, after some time, stole my heart and became my lifetime partner. Well, I should say, I thanked this immigration business of mine because it did not only brought me money. It also brought me the love of my life. She became the apple of my eye and the luck in all my other businesses.

At the age of 27, I had already experienced a lot of ups
and downs to continue succeeding in life.

This time, allow me to share how I knew and learned how to love beyond what I can show, do, and give to a person, not the same as the love that I have for my family. I now agreed with the most-used quote about love, which says that love moves in mysterious ways and that when it hits you, it will really hit you very hard. These things happened to me. Cupid's arrow was directly placed into the very core of my heart. The feeling was really different. It is indescribable.

I totally agree with Deb Caletti when she said, ***"The magic of purpose and of love in its purest form. Not television love, with its glare and hollow and sequined glint, not sex and allure, all high shoes and high drama, everything both too small and in too much excess, but just love. Love like rain, like the smell of tangerine, like a surprise found in your pocket."*** These words exactly described what I felt for her. She became my new source of inspiration and my added list of motivations.

This is our story. My wife applied for the job in April. When I first saw her, I did not feel that what they call "love at first sight." I was professional when I interviewed her. Knowing that I am very busy, I kept on traveling. Then, I went to India so, you could clearly say, I did not have any plan for her, and I did not want to risk it. I have not felt in love with anyone before. I just poured all my love to my parents and my dreams. I did not even know how it felt to be in love. I had no idea how to feel being cared for by someone special. I have not even tried liking someone before, even when I moved to the city and then to another bigger city, and then here in New Zealand. Well, to be very honest and prank, there were a few ladies who tried seducing me before with their beauty and body, most especially during the time when my businesses started to boom. They kept on messaging me, asking if we could go out and have a fun night, and also trying to befriend me, but I did not show any interest at all. I know what they really wanted. I know it so clearly. Their actions and moves speak it all. How could I expect they would love me until the end? What if one day, I get to lose everything? Will they still love me? Will they still choose me over the other bachelors in the world? My mother once told me before that I could not be looking for my partner because she will come to me at the right place and at the right time. That partner will also be the right person. I even told my mom that whenever I get to marry soon, I wanted a woman like her. I see my mom while growing up as a perfect example of a wife and a mother. I also dreamed of having a woman in my life, the same qualities as my mom. My mom knows how to cook meals, not just that, but good home-cooked meals. She takes good care of my dad very well. While growing up, my mom never failed to wipe the sweat of my father on the forehead. She never failed to say the words, "I love You," to him every day. She never failed to prepare coffee and food for him. She never failed to care for my dad. She never failed to forgive my dad for all his mistakes. Lastly, she never failed to love my dad, despite all the challenges they have been through. As a mother, my mom never failed to take care of us. She made sure we could eat, sleep, study, and enjoy every day. She taught us every value she could just to lead us to the right path. She has been an epitome of wisdom and love. Oh how, I missed my mom, again. Well, I am not saying that all these characteristics should be present but at least a few of them. However, my mom told me this, *"You cannot choose whom to love. Love will come to you in the most unexpected way, in the most unexpected time, and from the most unexpected person. Sometimes, they are just around you, maybe at your side, maybe at your back, she could be anywhere. But, be ready, when you love, be ready to get hurt, but I swear, it is a wonderful feeling to be in love."* Remembering those words, I could not thank my mom enough because even about love, she shared her thoughts about it with me. They even asked the last time I visited India if I already have someone special in my heart, but I immediately answered back that she did not come yet, with a big smile on my face. Going back, my wife still never gave up. As I said, she applied since April. But then, she sort of forced me and then she kept chasing on me, asking about the job. She contacted me the whole time and asked if she could join me in the office. She applied for the job in April, but until October, she did not leave me alone. She kept chasing me out, but I had no intention of being mad on my employee, but then, despite all the bothersome things she did, she has been a hardworking lady, and she only had a work visa. My impressions about her changed. She really is hard working. I did not know what was in her brain. Still, initially, she did not attract me, but as we came closer, worked together, and more and more situations that came along, I became more affectionate towards her. I did not know why. Maybe because we were always together at work, or maybe because

I see myself or my mom in her. Physically, she has a beautiful face with a charming smile. She's very lovely, but as I said, I was not attracted to her the very first time I saw her, but now, she has become more and more and more beautiful in my eyes. Being hardworking really attracts me the most. After hearing her life story, I felt pity for her. She also had a hard time in her life, just like what I had experienced. She came from a poor family, too. She came here to New Zealand to find a greener pasture and to get a good and stable job. She underwent lots of hurdles, too, just to be here and just to sustain her needs. Then, all that carried on. Aside from working hard, we kept talking and sharing everything about us. We also eat together, most especially during lunch. Basically, we are learning each other's life and knowing one another, better and better every single day. Everything was just filled with love. Which was very nice. That, for me, is the major event in my life. It was one big part of my memories that is worthy of a million times and reasons for remembering. My love for her is truly like a journey. Starting at forever. And ending at never. Right there and then, I knew she is the one. One night, I could not sleep. I tried closing my eyes, but still, I felt like I wanted to see someone else, and that was her. I wanted to be with her. I thought of it many, many, many times. I had so many questions in my mind. Some of them are these. ''If I ask her to marry me, would she say yes? Will she choose me? Am I fast or what? Is this already the right time? Will my parents approve my plan?'' So many questions in my mind. I told myself, just like my style in attacking businesses, I must have great plans for it. And so, I made my plans. One plan I should be making first is bringing her to India and let my parents know her. I will introduce them to her. If she would like my family, then it would be a plus. That only means she is very willing to love the people I also love. So, the next morning, I asked her to come with me to India. When she heard of it, she was very happy, excited, but at the same time, she said she's somewhat afraid. She told me she did not know if my parents and my whole family will like her. I assured her that my family is good. My family is composed of good people. And so, we travelled through-plane going to India. When we reached our small town, she looked pale. I held her hand, and I was shocked when it was very cold. She did feel nervous at that time. She even said she could pee because of nervousness. So, I told her that I will not leave her, that I will always be with her, in the whole duration of time that we will be in the village. Because of that, she finally smiled. Back home, my parents already knew that we were coming. In the house, they made a banner that has these letters, W-E-L-C-O-M-E H-O-M-E. Everyone was home. My siblings, my aunts, my cousins, and even my uncles who went overseas. It was their vacation time, too. What perfect timing, but for her, it was frightening because many are looking at her. When we arrived, my mom directly approached us. She hugged both of us.

Then we went to Rajni's place in Jalandhar to get together with our families. I know all my family members wanted to crack some jokes to me that finally, I already have my special someone. Still, I know they were just trying to keep their mouth shut and wait for me to introduce my lovely companion. Finally, she spoke. But the only word that came out from her mouth was the word, "Hi!" with a smile on her face. All my family members greeted back by saying "hello" with smiles on their faces, as well. Well, you don't know this, but I swear, my wife's smile is contagious, very cheerful and charming to watch. Right there and then, we started talking. We ate great food, different foods that we had not tasted before when we were still young. The memories before kept bringing back to me. When we ate, I could remember every single thing that usually happened before when we ate on one long table with several chairs in it. Topics for chit-chatting were limited. It was pure fun and memorable. Also, I get to introduce her to them. I narrated all of them about our love story. That includes how we met, how we learned that we already fell in love, how we started dating, how we decided to be with each other, and all that stuff. After that, my sisters made a tour for my wife in the house while I had a serious talk with my parents. I sort of had to convince my family to marry her. My mother asked me these exact words, "Are you very sure now of your decision? Do you think she's the one? My last question would be, are you happy with her? Because if you are, then, no need for you to ask for our approval. To be very honest, I could see so much love in your eyes, and it is reflected in your smile and in your actions. You are already at the right age, my son, and you deserve to be happy. Go on with your decision. We are here for you." Then my father added, "I know that you know what you are exactly doing. For as long as you are happy, rest assured that we are with you. For all these years, you have spent your life working for us and for our dreams. It is now time for you to settle down and be happier. You need not worry now of what to feed to your soon-to-be family, you need not worry now to pay for fees for their education, you need not worry now if they get soaked with the rain or if they get tanned with the scorching heat of the sun. You have prepared so much for it, my son. We are always here to support you." Those words brought me into tears. Even if I was already at the right age at that time, asking for approval or permission from my parents was really something for me. I could not afford to marry a woman my parents would not accept. My parents were my first love. I felt so happy knowing that my parents liked her, too. For a week's vacation in India, my wife had shown good attributes already to my family. She had learned to get along with them. She's very kind, respectful, helpful, and honest. Name it, my wife has it all. I just really feel so lucky to have her in my life. She's the greatest blessing I have ever had. Then, we flew back to New Zealand. We had to be back to our normal life. Many papers and reports were waiting for me there. Good thing, I had left my business with the right people while I was away. Also, at that time, we were adults. We knew what we're doing, and I guess she would have taken her time. She thought about things and me. I thought about her, as well. We took our time for six months. Yes, it took us six months to get married and settle down. We used to work in the same office. We took lunch together every day. We talked a lot. We really got attracted to each other. More and more every day. Everything has happened. Then, we got married. We finally tied the knot. She became mine. I became his. By that time, in terms of business life, we have an immigration business. We have the Botanic HealthCare. Things happened very well. We had Botanic Healthcare in India, USA, and New Zealand. We also recently bought Restaurants and Hotel Chain Coriander's in New Zealand. I also handle the SONI Real Estate group and provide residence and light commercial properties to sell and for rent. I also let my father manage the Tiling business in India to keep him busy.

In terms of money and other stuff, we just really exerted so much hard work for those things.

When it comes to doing business, we are always eager to make things going in the right direction, which makes our businesses grow.

This is the Coriander's Restaurants and Hotel Chain in New Zealand

This is the Botanic HealthCare.

Chapter VI

A Family Man

We finally got engaged on January 15, 2016, and got married on November 11, of the same year. We were very happy. During our wedding, my whole family was there, so as her family. We held our traditional wedding in India, and did traditional wedding practice. We were just also grateful because both families are very supportive. They helped us in the entire preparation. My sisters were on top of the other creative stuff. All my cousins were there, too. I forgot to share that they already got married. They got married a few years ago. They were happy, too, with their marriages. Before the wedding, days back, they talked to me. They advised me a few tips about married life. Of course, they have the guts to do that because they married earlier than I do. They said that no marriage is perfect. There are times you are both, there are also times you feel like the world is falling apart. But in the end, you have to remember that you are already one now. Two that became one. Two that are united as one. Let no person or thing separate you, but death alone. The topic and the ambiance were already kind of adulating for us, but that's already the reality. I thanked them for being great cousins to me. They never changed since we were still kids. And so, our wedding day came. It was held in one of the resorts in Punjab, and Rajni's family organized it. The venue was just so perfect for the celebration. Everyone in the place dressed beautifully. I was wearing a cream-white suite with Punjabi jutti. I preferred to wear all white to look clean and very formal.

She was gracefully walking down the aisle. Her white long bridal gown has shaped her body well, and her make-up was just natural. Her beauty really radiated as the ray of the sun hit her. While looking at her and waiting for her to reach the point where I was waiting, I just could not help myself but be in awe of her gorgeous appearance. My wife is very beautiful. Minutes after, the ceremony started. Then, we said our wedding vows to each other. Aside from the challenging moments I had encountered in my life, this one, meeting my wife and being with her is equally important with those challenges. So, allow me to share with you the exact message I said to her during our wedding vow. I want you all to know how much I love my wife.

This is how it goes....

To my beautiful wife, I did not know what the world means until I saw you. I did not know what love means until I met you. I did not know what happiness means until I loved you. Thank you for adding color to my life and for bringing light into my being. You taught me that any person can love unconditionally, even without asking something in return.

To my wife, you have become **my everything**. Now that we are married, I would like to ask you these things:

Please love me again whenever I am no longer lovable.

Please forgive me again whenever I am no longer forgivable.

Please understand me again whenever I am no longer understandable.

Lastly, you know my flaws, you know my imperfections, but thank you for choosing me to be with you, forever and ever. May you always choose me every day, every minute, every hour. Just as how I choose and love you every moment of my life. I love you very much, my lovely wife!

When I delivered those words, my wife hugged and kissed me. She cried. She felt so emotional with the things I said, but those things were not only filled with beautiful and flowering words. I meant to say every single word that came out from my mouth, and my wife knew that. My family knew that, as well, because I have been frank with everybody, and I always make true of the words I say. On the other hand, my wife also expressed her vow. My heart somewhat melted with joy. Her words were very touching. I did not expect she appreciated everything about me and how she wished me to be mine. Now, we are finally together, as one. And so, we had a party after that. Everyone danced and enjoyed the moment. All our parents and siblings gave short messages to us, so us our closest friends. That was a moment of a lifetime. We could never forget that. I could never forget that. Our dreams of success as husband and wife were also very fresh in my mind. We dreamt of living a simple and happy life. We dreamt of continuous blessings from the businesses we have. We dreamt of having kids. We dreamt of sending our kids to good and renowned schools. We dreamt of teaching our kids good values, just like how our parents taught us. We dreamt of having a happy and understanding marriage. It has been four years since we got married, and I am proud to say that these dreams are being made into a reality, day by day.

These are some of our wedding photos.

Another great blessing that came into our life was when my wife got pregnant. When I knew it, the typical reaction of an incoming father is also what I did. I immediately shouted, "I am now going to be a father." I kissed my wife, and I hugged her. I was so happy at that time. My wife is very excited, too. Imagine, we get to have our mini me or mini her already. I directly called back home and spread the good news. Everyone was very excited, too. My parents could not help but worry and advised us a lot of things to follow to keep our baby safe. I decided to hire a maid who could attend to the needs of my wife whenever I am at work. I already asked her to stop helping me in the immigration business, in the meantime, because I did not want her to feel stressed with things. Good thing, she also agreed with it. I always accompanied her to the gynecologist whenever she'll have her monthly check-up. I made sure I would not miss any time seeing our little bundle of joy, even if the baby is still in her tummy. Months pass by, the sex of the baby will already be revealed. I was so happy when they said to me that it is a boy. I said it's going to be my mini me. Later on, my wife gave birth. We have our son. His name is Tavish. He's our very first child. When I first saw Tavish, my reaction was indescribable. My tears fell down from my eyes. My happiness was just so immeasurable. Indeed, the feeling is just so different when you get to have your own child. I now understand better why my father and my mother did their very best to take good care of us. I now understand how much pain they experienced when I was far from home. I now understand how much they missed me when I can only go home and visit them sometimes. I now understand why they became so selfless for us. Since my wife needed me while she's recovering from giving birth, and also she needed assistance in taking care of my son, I assigned people to take over some work in the offices. I decided to work at home to be able to spend more time with my little boy and my wife. I know how much pain my wife exerted and gave when she gave birth to our son. All I could do to at least lessen the pain she felt, was to be with her. Both of us are first-time parents, so I thank my parents and her family for visiting us to help us take care of our Tavish. My little boy is now growing very well. He already knows a few things. He talks a few words, and he's been very sweet to us. Going back, a half year later, my wife got pregnant again. That time, we wished the baby would be a girl, so we'll already have a good pair. However, whatever sex our baby will have, we will still pour out to him or her our love and care just want we are giving and doing with Tavish. Months passed by, we had gender reveal again, and so, it was revealed that it's a girl. My wife and I were very happy. Now, it is already a match. We named her Sargam. She's very beautiful. Our Tavish is also very handsome. A year after, I had to be back in the field already. Working at home is far way different from working in the actual field. So, I definitely came back to my normal life. Been very busy with work. Days passed by, both of our kids were growing well and also, our businesses were going, too. We were also able to buy a new house after our wedding. The house we bought was our dream house. It is huge enough for our families when they come and visit us. I also built a mansion for my parents. They are living a good life now. They are now enjoying the life they have not experienced before. I just feel the contentment every time I go to bed and think of my parents, knowing that I need not worry about their food and shelter anymore. They are now staying in a mansion and everything that they need is just around them. They have servants too. I feel at peace sleeping at night, knowing that my family is living a comfortable life. It is a great reward for all the sacrifices that have been through in the past. As of now, I am into property, nutrition supplements, immigration, hospital business. I just feel so happy because my wife is always there to support me. Since I am very busy, my wife gets to take care of the kids. My wife is a very affectionate lady. I am just so lucky to have her. She's also very caring. She would always cope up with me. So, when I am at home. I make sure I cope up with my family. I make sure I still have time for my wife and for my kids. I used to play with my kids. We make sure every day that we treat them fairly and love them as much as they could. The ages that they have right now deserve so much attention, and it is at that age that they start appreciating and learning things.

I do not want my kids to grow wanting to have to opposite life. I do not want them to wish or get jealous of other families. That is why, despite my hectic schedule, I always find time to make out with them. It takes a lot of effort, but I have to do it to become an effective father. As much as we can, my wife and I already started training our kids with good values. I want us to be like my father and mother. Even if we were not rich years back, still, we were rich with value and love from them. That, I should say, is very priceless, and I could never exchange that memory with anything. Day by day, to be very honest, we are striving to become no the best parents in the whole wide world but to become good parents worth emulating by our children.

These are our photos with Tavish and Sargam on their birthday.

Chapter VII

It is time for paying it forward

"*Paying it forward is about caring and sharing. It is about compassion and kindness. It is about generosity. It is about sacrifice and love. You get what you give, so give good.*"

This beautiful saying is a great reflection of my story and how I was able to give back to the people or places who have contributed a lot to who I am today. I just could not imagine that after how many years of facing hurdles and giving sacrifices, finally, I have reached what I want to become. I am now a different version of LIEK GAURAV. I became who I am today because I did not give up during difficult times, and I always observed hard work. More importantly, I was loaded with several bullets of dreams and goals in life.

In terms of historical events, I could say I have always been attached to my roots, the joint family I was with, and the village I came from. My hometown, which is a very small town, I could never forget its beauty. When I was young, I had a secret dream, which is to give back to society when I grow up. To my town, I desired to do good things about it. I loved the place I came from. The provincial life always keeps coming back to my memories. The way we lived before was so simple but, we were also happy. We enjoyed small stuff and learned to appreciate small things. My hometown had honed me to be braver when I came to the city life. My hometown became my basis and my inspiration, so as the people in it, in defeating loneliness and nothingness. A lot of people said and suggested that I could go to other big cities or even countries. I can go wherever I want to go. I can bring my family to where they want me.

We can afford to travel anywhere now, but I just don't know why I loved our small town. There is nothing like it. The air and the atmosphere are just so refreshing. Everything is also clean and green. Everybody also knows us. Our family was wealthy, my grandparents, and my uncles. It's just that, my father was a poor man. It was very hard because we had to maintain the standards of money, but we did not have money. When my kids grow, I will surely bring them always to my hometown. I would show them where we usually take a shower, where we feed our animals, where we walk going to school, where we play basketball, where we eat together, where we brush our teeth, where we make our home works, and where I first got muddy. I would also introduce them to all the people in the village. I am pretty sure they would also love and appreciate provincial life, just like I do.

Talking about my upbringing, in terms of morale and etiquette, the mother has given us good manners and etiquette. We value money well. We value keeping others safe and not hurting them. We value being honest and being loyal. We value being true and not cheating other people. All those things made us very good human beings. This is because we are people of good values. People would tell my mom that her kids are really good. Manners and etiquettes are incomparable. They also added that they have not seen kids like us. My mother gives importance to values. We learned to be sensible, too. Well, these are very evident in me. No one ever complained about my nature, my personality, my morale, my hard work, my eagerness, my capability to learn things, and everything. I should say, the joint family I was accustomed to really help me a lot with my character. I also learned not to make dramas and not making issues. My father, on the other hand, has taught me hard work and discipline. Could you still remember when I shared about rules imposed by my mother about waking up early, doing my homework and studying my lessons, taking care of the animals, consuming food which we can only eat, and all other stuff which is life-related. I am very proud to say that my parents are my real treasures. They are not just my inspiration. They are my life. In their own simple way, they tried their very best to provide for our needs, even if they needed to give blood and sweat for us. They are my great influencers. They influenced my way of seeing life in itself and my way of handling things. I will forever thank them, and I will never get tired of doing it.

Now, in terms of work, expect me to be very professional. I always require good performance from everybody working with me. I do not want to have lazy employees. I want everything to be passed early. Deadlines should always be met on time. I also want respect to be embraced in the workplace that we are in. However, I am a totally different man when I work outside. I am a mellow guy. I am funny. I am funky. My wife tells me how somebody could believe that I am a person like this when I am not in the office when I am not in a suit. At home, I can just be just snickers. I am just a very plain guy and very pure. I am just very simple. I am not very fancy. I mean, I can have one pair of shoes for seven years if they keep going. I would not bother, but my passion is eagerness. It is a business. It is doing business. It is doing hard work. In terms of humor, there's nothing so much more to add. I have always been a serious guy. But, I am also quite naughty as well. I always keep taking risks and then move on. In trusting bits about being me as a person, wherever I go, whoever I go business with, people tell me that they get positive vibes. The moment they talk to me and the moment they come around me, they always say that I am the right person to do business with. They say that I am the right person to trust. They say I am the right person to partner with. They say I am the right person to get friendship with. It is just pure positivity. I could not recall if I thought about anything negative in my life. My mind is filled with ideas about family, work, kids, business, and parents. There is really no negativity at all. I just really do not think about the negative. What I always think of is positive. I guess that is something that kept me going, all along, because I do not get distracted with "What Ifs." You see? My personalities really changed when I am in a different place or situation or when I am with different people. It really depends, but I swear I am not wearing any mask at all. What you hear and what you see is really me. Every single day, I am showing off to all the real me. No pretensions, no hiding.

Talking about my significance, in the whole society, and in the whole world, I have built a perfect name. Again, I would just like to make things clear, and I have repeated this many times, I am not bragging. I am telling the truth. I was able to build a good name because I worked hard for it. I am a very knowledgeable guy because I studied a lot, and I never stopped learning. Every day, everywhere, every hour, I learn. I am doing my best to also learn something new, always. I have formulated a lot of good dietary supplements and nutraceutical botanical extract ventures for all. I have truly built a good name in the said industry. People keep coming back and forth to patronize our product because, aside from seeing my life an inspiration, they see my product very beneficial to them, and that is something to be thankful for. I take pride in what I do. Being an immigration adviser, I am quite a known figure. Everybody knows me. Everybody knows me in India, in New Zealand, and in other areas. This is because of immigration work and my other businesses. Others know me dealing that I am with more than 500 people and 500 e-mails a day all over the world. People could identify me of how much significance I brought to the community. Back home, in India, I always look after people, most especially the poor ones. Whenever I go back home, people love it. People want to talk to me. People want to see me. People want to sit around with me, but I am always busy, but in order for them to not feel bad, I always throw a small gathering where everyone gets to see me and eat good food and build wonderful memories. Even kids in our place also want to talk to me. They know a bit of my story because their parents told them so, and they made me as their role model in reaching success. I feel happy about that. At least, at a very young age, their dreams are already alive and kicking. And of course, I also want to witness those kids, to be like me in the future. I even want them to be better than me because I know that they can.

In terms of my personal qualities, I have always been a positive person. Optimism became my drive. I am a smart guy. I have always been desperate to achieve things. There should always be no room for error. That is why I keep on planning and planning and planning things before executing them. I have always been a person who loves to do things better and better. I don't wait for one thing to finish and start. I just go behind things. I just get things done. And that is what my specialization is now. Being the CEO of the companies, my specialization is to solve problems. I am very good at execution. If somebody has a problem, we just go and fix things out.

If it's about the actions and the life events which bring out the qualities and objectives in me, I guess one of the very important things is that my mother trained me before to be responsible and independent. I have shared this earlier, but I will share this again. She had given me responsibility quite early in my life. She used to give me phone bills, which I need to deposit them. I had to stand on the line. And I guess, my sense of responsibility came from those days. We were in a joint family, and then, obviously, my father was not a rich

man. He's a very plain and clear person. He's not smart. All the responsibility was on my mother's shoulder, and we have to help her out. Those qualities came from our life-events and the upbringing they shared with us, from a poor and desperate environment. My parents never get tired of keeping and preparing us to be on the right path.

The life events that I have explained about my childhood, my schooling, and the desperate actions to make a living have shaped me as a person, of who I am today. Also, the positivity, the drive to achieve things. It is not about money. It is just about doing things. Clearing opportunities for others. Yes, I would create a business for us, but then, it is all about being the boss. It is all about driving the business and get the stuff done by people, which I think the quality which people lack.

In terms of obstacles or take risks, I think I was able to handle everything pretty well. I don't think I happened to be lucky. Everything that I earned has always been bloody hard work, and I think that is what I enjoyed the most. I worked hard for everything I have now. If it is not hard work, it could not have been more enjoyable. What I achieved is making and transforming a person with no investment, no family support, and no industry to someone who already has everything. Now, I am a multi-billion-dollar person with lots of factories in India. I have hotels and restaurants. I am into hospitality.

I also have a tiling factory back home. Obviously, I want to make my mom and dad proud, so I built a very nice mansion. It is a massive house, just to make them proud, and I have a house for myself. I have a good quality home. I purposely built a tile factory in the village

I came from so people could get jobs. I wanted to remind people that I am the guy who started the factory, and I guess to all that I achieved, after so many years, with my parents being poor. My family all depends on me. I am the only one supporting them and making money. The kind of support that I give to my parents is admired by many people all over the world. They wanted to have a son like me, who still look after his parents. AT home, they already have a good life now. They have servants. They need not work hard in heat and rain. They also come over to New Zealand to visit us here. Then, life is just a happy life. For me, having a wife and two kids, my parents, my family back home, and a lot of businesses, no trouble. Life is great. Very busy it is, but every day, things are going and growing. We are achieving things together, and that is because of hard work, persistence, and eagerness.

This is me at age 29. Success cannot be determined by age, as long as you are willing to strive harder to reach your goals.

My autobiography is not as brilliant as the autobiographies of other well-known people. Still, I swear, you will learn a lot of things after reading it. To my joint family back home, thank you for the things you have imprinted in me. To my parents, thank you for raising me well. To my wife, thank you for loving me undoubtedly. To my two lovely children, thank you for giving me the chance to become your father. May you be proud of what I have become!

And to you, who are reading this story of mine, may you get a reason to work for your dreams, no matter how hard it could be and no matter where it could lead you. I was able to nail things, I know, you also can!

Printed in the United States
By Bookmasters